PENGUIN BOOKS
GREEN POEMS

Gulzar, one of India's leading poets, is a greatly respected scriptwriter and film director. He has been one of the most popular lyricists in mainstream Hindi cinema, gaining international fame when he won an Oscar and a Grammy for the song 'Jai Ho'. Gulzar received the Sahitya Akademi Award in 2002, the Padma Bhushan in 2004, the Dadasaheb Phalke Award in 2014 and the Jnanpith Award in 2024. He lives and works in Mumbai.

Writer-diplomat Pavan K. Varma is a graduate in history from St Stephen's College (securing the first position in the college), after which he took a degree in law from the University of Delhi. He joined the Indian Foreign Service in 1976. A well-known translator and writer of depth and insight, he has written over a dozen bestselling books, including *Adi Shankaracharya: Hinduism's Greatest Thinker*. He lives in Delhi.

BY THE SAME AUTHOR

Selected Poems, translated by Pavan K. Varma
100 Lyrics, translated by Sunjoy Shekhar
Neglected Poems, translated by Pavan K. Varma
Half a Rupee: Stories, translated by Sunjoy Shekhar
Yudhishtar and Draupadi, translation of a work
by Pavan K. Varma
Triveni, translated by Neha R. Krishna
Actually . . . I Met Them
89 Autumns of Poems: Selected, Neglected, Suspected

green poems

GULZAR

Translated by PAVAN K. VARMA

PENGUIN BOOKS

An imprint of Penguin Random House

PENGUIN BOOKS

Penguin Books is an imprint of the Penguin Random House group of companies
whose addresses can be found at global.penguinrandomhouse.com

Published by Penguin Random House India Pvt. Ltd
4th Floor, Capital Tower 1, MG Road,
Gurugram 122 002, Haryana, India

First published by Penguin Books India 2014
This edition published in Penguin Books by Penguin Random House India 2025

ISBN 9780143422822

Typeset in Sabon by Eleven Arts, Delhi
Printed at Replika Press Pvt. Ltd, India

www.penguin.co.in

Dedication

Justice Najmi Waziri

At least a million trees wave their leaves for him in gratitude, in Delhi!

His relentless work to protect the enviroment of Delhi remained untold

I take a bow to you, Sir.

Gulzar

Contents

Contents

Contents

Contents

Contents

Foreword

Green Poems is Gulzar's lyrical and sensitive tribute to nature in all its many-splendoured facets. I have always maintained that Gulzarsaab's poetic oeuvre is very extensive. It encompasses love, sorrow, joy, grief, human relationships, the ordinary and the extraordinary, and the daily, unnoticed and often remarkable minutiae of the ebb and flow of life. Nothing really escapes his relentlessly observing poetic eye. As part of this extensive canvas, nature has remained his consistent and sustained passion.

In writing about nature, Gulzar gives to it a personality of its own. He does not so much write *about* it as he writes through it, allowing it to speak. In this process he is both an observer and a participant in its joys and travails. For him, a river or a cloud or a mountain, a tree or a leaf or the sky and the universe beyond are not objects of observation, but living, animate beings with a soul and a purpose and a will distinct from that of the observer. He is then in dialogue with them, combining humour and pathos and irony and great beauty in his compositions.

Interestingly, in Gulzar's poetic lexicon, it is human beings who are very often the objects of observation for nature. Instead of being the observed, nature becomes the observer of our finite and puny worlds and our myriad irrelevant preoccupations. The dexterity with which he crafts this process simultaneously brings out both the majesty of nature and, by sheer contrast, the limitations of human vanity and endeavour.

Foreword

Beyond the exquisite play of words, *Green Poems* is also a testament to a poet's abiding concern about what we as human beings are doing to nature. As a poet, Gulzar would arguably rank among the most effective and genuine voices of environmental conservation and of the need to give respect to the natural world. He writes of this world fully conscious of what human ambition and greed are doing to it. The world is fragile for him, perennially endangered, forever held hostage to our effortless ability to unthinkingly desecrate it, unmindful of the consequences this can unleash on our own long-term well-being. *Green Poems* is thus a poetic text that reinforces the work of professional environmentalists. In my view, it should become a prescribed text in schools and educational institutions to bring home the message of environmental preservation, taking this vitally important area beyond merely academic and professional concern.

As always, translating Gulzarsaab's poetry has been a delight. It would be an understatement for me to say that he is a poet for whom I have the highest respect. In fact, I think he is one of the greatest poets of our time. In addition, of course, he is a wonderful human being and, by now, one of my closest friends. We have now worked together on three translated volumes of his poems: *Selected Poems*, *Neglected Poems* and this latest book. I consider myself very privileged that Gulzarsaab has, on his part, translated into Hindustani one of my works, *Yudhishtar and Draupadi*. Ours is a literary connection enriched by a hugely rewarding personal relationship. May he continue to write for another hundred years!

Pavan K. Varma

Introduction

Some dry leaves dropped from the tree. The season was changing. But the rustle of the leaves had something more to say. I heard them. What they said was profound, to save the globe from rotting.

'Save the environment and keep the globe green,' they said.

I have heard many a leaf—and trees, rivers, mountains and waterfalls. I am relating their stories to people in poems. Hence I decided to call this collection *Green Poems*.

My gratitude to Pavanji for his translations into English; he has always been very kind to the poets. And a special thanks to Udayan Mitra for pruning and shaping and gardening the Green Poems.

Gulzar

एक अकेला पत्ता !

सर—सब्ज चेहरा उसका,
दो रोज से पीला है
छू जाये हवा का झोंका तो वो काँपने लगता है

जिस पेड़ पे लटका है,
वो आधा डूब चुका है अब सैलाब के पानी में
कितना पानी और चढ़ेगा पता नहीं

वो एक अकेला पत्ता,
पेड़ से कहता जाता है
तू डरना मत... मैं हूँ ना!
तू डरना मत... मैं हूँ ना!

गुलजार

A Leaf left Alone

Its lush green face
Has paled in the last two days
It begins to tremble if a gust of wind touches it

The tree from which it hangs
Is half-drowned in the flood waters
No one knows how much higher the water will rise!

That one leaf
Keeps telling the tree
Don't be afraid, I'm there!
Don't be afraid, I'm there!

GREEN POEMS

मुंह ही मुंह कुछ बुड़बुड़ करता, बहता रहता है दरिया।

मुंह ही मुंह कुछ बुड़बुड़ करता, बहता रहता है दरिया
छोटी छोटी ख़्वाहिशें हैं कुछ उसके दिल में . . .
रेत पे रेंगते रेंगते सारी उम्र कटी है,
पुल पर चढ़ के बहने की ख़्वाहिश है दिल में!

जाड़ों में जब कोहरा उसके पूरे मुंह पर आ जाता है
और हवा लहरा के उसका चेहरा पोंछ के जाती है
एक दफ़ा तो वो भी उसके साथ उड़े
और जंगल से ग़ायब हो जाए!

कभी कभी यूं भी होता है
पुल से रेल गुज़रती है तो बहता दरिया, पल की पल बस रुक
    जाता है
इतनी सी उम्मीद लिए . . .
शायद फिर से देख सके वो, इक दिन उस लड़की का चेहरा,
जिसने फूल और तुलसी उसको पूज के अपना वर मांगा था . . .

उस लड़की की सूरत उसने,
अक्स उतारा था जब से, तह में रख ली थी!!

The River

Muttering to himself the river flows along
Some small desires still alive in his heart
An entire life spent slithering along the sand
Now he wants to climb up and flow over the bridge!

In winter, when the fog settles all over his face
And the wind flutters by wiping his countenance clean
He wants, just once, to soar along with the breeze
And simply vanish from the forest.

Sometimes, when a train passes over the bridge
The flowing river stops momentarily
With one wish
Maybe to see once again that girl's face
Who had offered flowers and tulsi to him
For the good husband to find.

That image of the girl's face
Caught as a reflection
It has retained deep within!

सितंबर

सितंबर के दिनों में . . .
आसमां हर साल ही बीमार रहता है
एलर्जी है कोई शायद . . .

सितंबर आते ही बारिश का पानी सूखने लगता है और
बादल के टुकड़े, मैले गंदे पोतड़ों
जैसे पड़े रहते हैं, रूखी, चिड़चिड़ी सी धूप में दिन भर . . .

छपाकी सी निकल आती है, शाम होते ही सारी पीठ पर
और लाल हो जाता है इक हिस्सा फ़लक का जैसे ज़हरीले
    किसी बिच्छू ने काटा हो।

कई दिन खांसता है आसमां और लाल, काली आंधी चलती है
बहुत बीमार रहता है सितंबर के दिनों में आसमां मेरा!

September

In September
The sky remains ill every year
It has some kind of allergy, perhaps . . .

The moment September arrives the rains begin to
    shrivel up
Pieces of clouds, like dirty, soiled nappies,
Lie around in the dry, irritable sunshine.

By dusk, a rash breaks out on the sky's back
And a patch of the sky, as if stung by a poisonous scorpion,
Becomes an angry red.

For many days a cough wracks the sky,
A crimson dark wind swirls around;
My sky in September remains very unwell!

मनाली

बड़ी मासूम लगती थी . . .
पतंगों की तरह उड़ती हुई जब बर्फ़ उतरी थी

परिंदे हैरां हैरां से
ज़रा सी चोंच खोले देखते थे,
न पर, न आंख, न मुंह है
भला कैसे पतंगे हैं
पकड़ लो तो हवा की एक गीली बूंद है, जो मुंह में आती है!

बड़ी चुपचाप लेकिन रात भर गिरती रही वो बर्फ़ वादी में
न बारिश की तरह गरजी,
न दरवाज़ा किसी का खटखटाया, न किसी खिड़की पे दस्तक दी . . .
किसी की नींद पर पांव नहीं रखा,
किसी ख़ामोशी पर आहट नहीं फेंकी,
वो सारी रात बरसी थी . . .!

बड़ी पोली सी सुबह थी
फलों की टोकरी से बर्फ़ पर लुढ़कते हुए बच्चे,
तमाशे कर रहे थे,
कोई खिड़की कहीं देखो, वो आबी रंग में क्रिसमस का ग्रीटिंग
        कार्ड लगती थी
बेचारी खुश्क शाख़ों ने तो अपनी उंगलियों पर
पट्टियां सी बांध लीं रूई के कपड़े की . . .

6

Manali

The snow looked so innocent
When it came down
Like so many moths flying around.

The birds, taken aback,
Stared with their beaks half open
What they thought were moths without mouths, eyes
    or wings
Became, when caught, a drop of moisture in their mouth.

In complete silence the snow fell the entire night in the
    valley
No thunder as happens with rain
No door rattled, no window startled by a knock
No one woke up
No stillness was jostled
Quietly, it just snowed the whole night.

The morning looked so soft
Children rolled out of a fruit basket,
Slid about in the snow
Windows everywhere were like a Christmas card in water
    colours
The poor, bare tree branches
Scraped by autumn just two months ago.

अभी दो माह पहले ही उन्हें पतझड़ ने छीला था
बड़ी मासूम लगती थी, बरसती बर्फ़ की बारिश
मगर बेहिस भी लगती थी
न उसका स्वाद था कोई
न उस से चोट लगती थी
ज़रा सी ढीट लगती थी

मुसलसल आठवां दिन है
ज़मीं के पास पास उड़ते हुए काले परिंदे ढूंढ़ते हैं
कोई दाना, कोई पत्ता, कोई ख़ूराक का टुकड़ा,
कि दरियाओं ने भी मोटी सी चादर ओढ़ ली है बर्फ़ के मुंह पर
छतों ने 'हैट' में आंखें छुपा ली हैं
हवेली ने बड़ी सी एक गांधी टोपी पहनी है
हवा से बचने की ख़ातिर
हर इक दीवार ने कॉलर चढ़ाए हैं

बड़ा चालाक था ये बर्फ़ का हमला . . .
कि सब से पहले उसने खाने पीने के वसीले बंद कर डाले
पहाड़ों से फ़रार होन के दरों पर कई फ़ुट चौड़ी दीवारें बना डालीं
सभी 'शहराएं' बंद कर दीं . . .
सभी दरवाज़े फाटक, जाम कर डाले
बड़ी खूंख्वार है ये बर्फ़ जो इस शहर को लेकर हिरासत में खड़ी है
बड़ी मासूम लगती है . . .
बड़ी चंडाल निकली है!

Looked as if their fingers had cotton bandages on
The snow coming down in torrents appeared so innocent
But also without feeling or touch
It left no taste on the tongue
It couldn't hurt
It seemed just a little impudent.

It has now snowed for eight days continuously!
Black-looking birds hover low over the ground
Searching for a morsel, a leaf, anything to eat
Even the rivers have covered their faces
In a thick blanket of snow
Roofs have hidden their eyes under a hat
Mansions wear a large Gandhi cap
Walls have put up their collars
To protect themselves from the wind.

How clever was this assault of the snow
The first thing it did was to choke off all avenues to food
Passes that could provide an escape from the mountains
Blocked by walls several feet wide
The city squares are closed
Doors and entrances all jammed
How ruthless is this snow that has taken an entire town
    captive
It looked so innocent
It turned out to be so merciless!

चलो इन बादलों की सारी परतें छील के देखें . . .

चलो इन बादलों की सारी परतें छील के देखें
ज़रूर इन के लबादों में
कहीं पोशीदा जेबें भी लगी होंगी

टटोलें इनकी जेबें . . . और देखें
कहां पानी की बूंदें हैं?
कहां ओले छुपाए हैं?
कहां रखते हैं डमरू? जब बजाते हैं तो बच्चे चौंक जाते हैं

किसी इक 'बेल्ट' में बिजली का हंटर भी छुपा होगा
हवाओं के गुबारे भी भरे होंगे
तुम्हें लगता नहीं बादल बड़े शातिर मदारी हैं!

What the Clouds Conceal

Come, let us peel all the layers of these clouds
There are bound to be in their garments
Many hidden pockets attached.

Let us go through those pockets and discover
Where the drops of rain are.
Where are the hailstorms hidden?
Where do they keep the drums whose resounding startles
    children?

In some belt must be hidden the whiplash of lightning
Balloons full of gusts of wind too
Don't you think these clouds are very clever magicians?

एक नदी की बात सुनी . . .

एक नदी की बात सुनी
इक शायर से पूछ रही थी
रोज़ किनारे दोनों हाथ पकड़ के मेरे
सीधी राह चलाते हैं
रोज़ ही तो मैं
नाव भर कर, पीठ पे लेकर
कितने लोग हैं पार उतार के आती हूं

रोज़ मेरे सीने पे लहरें
नाबालिग़ बच्चों के जैसे
कुछ कुछ लिखती रहती हैं

क्या ऐसा हो सकता है जब
कुछ भी न हो
कुछ भी नहीं . . .
और मैं अपनी तेह से पीठ लगा के इक शब रुकी रहूं
बस ठहरी रहूं
जैसे कविता कह लेने के बाद पड़ी रह जाती है
मैं पड़ी रहूं . . .!

The Story of a River

There is the story of a river
Who inquired of a poet:
Every day my two banks hold me by my arms
And make me walk a given path;
And, every day, on my back, I carry
Boats full of people to the other side.

Every day, like adolescent children,
The waves write something on my chest.

Can it not be
That someday nothing happens
Nothing at all
And I put my back to my bed
And remain motionless for one evening
Just still
Like a poem lies inert after being read
Unmoving, at rest?

For Rekha Bharadwaj.

मैं जंगल से गुज़रता हूं तो लगता है मेरे पुरखे खड़े हैं!

मैं जंगल से गुज़रता हूं तो लगता है मेरे पुरखे खड़े हैं
मैं इक नौ ज़ाइदा बच्चा
ये पेड़ों के क़बीले
उठ के हाथ में मुझ को झुलाते हैं

कोई इक झुनझुना फूलों का हाथों से बजाता है
कोई आंखों पे पुचकाता है ख़ुशबुओं की पिचकारी
बहुत बूढ़ा सा दढ़ियल एक बरगद गोद में लेकर मुझे हैरान
                                        होता है, सुनाता है
तुम अब चलने लगे हो!
हमारे जैसे थे तुम भी, जड़ें मिट्टी में रहती थीं
बड़ी ताक़त लगाते थे तुम अपने बीज में सूरज पकड़ने की
ज़मीं पर आए थे पहले
तुम्हें फिर रेंगते देखा . . .
हमारी शाख़ों पर चढ़ते थे, चढ़ के कूद जाते थे,
                                        फुदकते थे
मगर दो पांव पर जब तुम खड़े होकर के दौड़े, फिर नहीं लौटे
पहाड़ों पत्थरों के हो गए तुम!

The Forest

When I pass through the forest it seems my ancestors
    are around me
I feel I am a newborn baby
And these tribes of trees
Are rocking me in their arms.

Some play a flower rattle, others sprinkle fragrance on
    my eyes
One very old, bearded *bargad*
Takes me in his lap, surprise writ on his face,
And tells me:
Now you have begun to walk
But once you too were like us
With your roots in the ground
Straining with all your might to catch the sun.
You had just arrived on earth
And I saw you slithering around,
On our branches you would climb, jump down again,
Scamper around
But once, standing on both legs, you could run
You did not return
You became a part of the rocks, of the mountains!

मगर फिर भी . . .
तुम्हारे तन में पानी है
तुम्हारे तन में मिट्टी है
हमीं से हो . . .
हमीं में फिर से बोए जाओगे, तुम फिर से लौटोगे!

But even so
The water in your body
The soil in your being
Is from us
You will be seeded again in us
You will return to us again.

दरख़्त सोचते हैं जब, तो फूल आते हैं

दरख़्त सोचते हैं जब, तो फूल आते हैं
वो धूप में डुबो के उंगलियां
ख़्याल लिखते हैं, लचकती शाख़ों पर
तो रंग रंग लफ़्ज़ चुनते हैं
खुशबुओं से बोलते हैं और बुलाते हैं

हमारा शौक़ देखिए . . .
कि गर्दनें ही काट लेते हैं
जहां कहीं महकता है कोई!

Trees

When trees pause to think, flowers bloom
Dipping their fingers in the sunshine
They write their thoughts on swaying branches
Picking their words in different hues of colour
They converse with fragrances and call us to them.

Look at our passion:
The moment anything emerges which is fragrant,
We chop off its neck!

पतझड़ में जब पत्ते गिरने लगते हैं . . .

पतझड़ में जब पत्ते गिरने लगते हैं
क्या कहते होंगे शाख़ों से?

हम तो अपना मौसम जी कर जाते हैं
तुम ख़ुश रहना—
तुम को तो हर मौसम की औलादें पाल के
रुख़्सत करनी होंगी

शाख़ की बारी आई थी जब कटने की
तो पेड़ से बोली . . . ख़ुद बोली थी
तुमको मेरी उम्र लगे . . .
तुम को तो बढ़ना है, और ऊंचा होना है
दूसरी आ जाएगी, मुझ को याद न रखना!

पेड़ ज़मीं से क्या कहता, जब खोद खोद कर
उस की जड़ों के टांके तोड़े
और ज़मीं से अलग किया!

उलटा ज़मीं को कहना पड़ा . . .
याद है इक छोटे से बीज से तुमने
     झांक के देखा था जब पहली पत्ती आई थी!
फिर आना, और मेरी कोख से पैदा होना,
गर मैं बची रही!!

20

Leaves in Autumn

When leaves fall in autumn
What do they say to the branches?

We have lived our season and must leave
But you must continue to prosper
You have to nurture the progeny of coming seasons
And bid them goodbye.

When the time came for the branch to be pruned
It said to the tree, addressing it directly:
May my years be added to yours
You have to grow, become even taller
Don't miss me, other branches will grow in my place.

What did the tree say to the earth
When the ground was mercilessly dug up, disjointing
    its roots
And uprooting it from the soil?

The earth itself was forced to say:
Remember, when as a tiny seed you peeped out
And saw the leaves when they first sprouted?
Come again, to be born in my womb
If I survive!

फ़िज़ा ये बूढ़ी लगती है।

फ़िज़ा ये बूढ़ी लगती है
पुराना लगता है मकां . . .

समंदर के पानियों से नील अब उतर चुका
हवा के झोंके छूते हैं तो खुरदरे से लगते हैं
बुझे हुए बहुत से टुकड़े आफ़ताब के,
जो गिरते हैं ज़मीं की तरफ़ तो ऐसा लगता है
कि दांत गिरने लग गए हैं बुड्ढे आसमां के!

फ़िज़ा ये बूढ़ी लगती है
पुराना लगता है मकां . . .!

This Ageing Earth

This earth looks aged
This house looks old.

The blue has faded from the waters of the sea
The gusts of wind appear dry and listless
The extinguished pieces of the sun
Fall towards the earth
Like teeth from the mouth of an ageing sky.

This earth looks aged
This house is no longer new.

मोड़ पे देखा है

मोड़ पे देखा है वो पेड़—सा इक पेड़ कभी?
मेरा वाक़िफ़ है, बहुत सालों से मैं उसे जानता हूं

जब मैं छोटा था तो इक आम उड़ाने के लिए
परली दीवार से कंधों पे चढ़ा था उसके
जाने दुखती हुई किस शाख़ से जा पांव लगा
धाड़ से फेंक दिया था मुझे नीचे उसने
मैंने खुन्नस में बहुत फेंके थे पत्थर उसपर

मेरी शादी पे मुझे याद है शाख़ें देकर
मेरी वेदी का हवन गर्म किया था उसने
और जब हामला थी 'बीबा' तो दोपहर में हर दिन
मेरी बीवी की तरफ़ कैरियां फेंकी थीं उसी ने

वक़्त के साथ सभी फूल, सभी पत्ते गए

तब भी जल जाता था जब मुन्ने से कहती 'बीबा'
'हां, उसी पेड़ से आया है तू, पेड़ का फल है'
अब भी जल जाता हूं, जब मोड़ गुज़रते में कभी
खांस कर कहता है, 'क्यूं, सर के सभी बाल गए?'

सुबह से काट रहे हैं वो कमेटी वाले
मोड़ तक जाने की हिम्मत नहीं होती मुझको!

The Tree at the Corner

Have you seen, at that corner, that ageing tree?
It is an acquaintance I have known for years.

When I was small I had climbed on to its shoulders
From the adjacent wall, to steal a mango
My feet touched one of its branches that was hurting
It threw me down with a thud
Angry, I threw many stones at it.

At my wedding, I remember, it gave its branches
To warm the fire for the havan
And when Beeba was pregnant
It threw, every afternoon,
Its raw mangoes at my wife.

With time, all its leaves and flowers disappeared.

I would be jealous when Beeba told the baby:
'You have come from that tree, you are his fruit.'
Even today I feel angry when, as I pass the turning, he
    coughs
And says: 'Hey, have you lost your hair?'

Today, since morning, the municipal authorities are
    cutting it to pieces
I do not have the courage to go up to the corner.

थंपू–भूटान

थंपू छू ———— (छू मतलब नदी)
तेरी बिरादरी की कुछ नदियां
मेरे यहां भी बहती हैं
ऐसे ही सैराब किया करती हैं ज़मीनें
ऐसे ही वो कश्तियां भर के, लोगों को
साहिल पार करा देती हैं

उनको फेंट के, कहीं कहीं, अब बिजली पैदा करने लगे हैं
शोर होता है
टूटते होंगे नदियों के लचकीले बदन

रात की ख़मोशी में लेकिन थंपू छू
कुछ जाप किया करती हो तुम
वो क्या है?
सागर संगम कहती हो या
फेंटे जाने से बचने की–
चुपचाप दुआएं करती हो?

Thimphu

Thimphu Chhu
Some rivers of your tribe flow too
From where I come
They flow around, just like you, make the land fertile
And fill up boats, just as you do
To take people to the other shore.

Sometimes, their waters are whipped to produce
    electricity
There is an outcry:
The delicate bodies of the rivers must be breaking!

In the silence of the night
There is something that you chant Thimphu Chhu
What is that?
Do you talk of your yearning to merge with the ocean
Or quietly pray
That you be saved the prospect of being whipped?

फ़रवरी

धुंधले धुंधले,
ड्रॉइंग बुक में बने हुए कुछ चारकोल के ख़ाके से
कोहरे में किरदार ये पेड़ों के कितने अच्छे लगते हैं

अमराई में सेठों जैसे
तोंद बढ़ा के बैठे हैं कुछ आमों वाले
टेक के पेड़ों के पत्ते तो रस्सियों पर लटके बच्चों के
                                    गीले पोतड़े लगते हैं
एक तरफ़ इक टोली ठहरी है कुछ झोली वाले नंग फ़क़ीरों की
इक नर्तकी दूर अकेली हाथ उठाए नाच रही है
इक छोटा सा, बौने क़द का
सर्कस वाले मसख़रे का सा
आर के लक्ष्मण के कार्टूनों के किरदार
शायद उड़ कर झाड़ियों में जा अटके हैं
हवा का झोंका छूता है तो रोल बदल जाते हैं इन किरदारों के
पोशाकें बदल कर लौट आते हैं

देर तलक रहता है कोहरा फ़रवरी में
फ़रवरी में पाला पड़ता है!!

February

Like the fading, hazy lines
Of charcoal portraits in a drawing book
How nice the profiles of these trees look in the fog.

Like affluent traders in the season of fruit
Some mango trees sit with their bellies bloated
The leaves of teak trees look like the wet clothes
Of children hanging from a rope.
A dancer, far in the distance, dances alone with her hands raised.
A small, dwarf-like character
Like a circus clown
Recalling the cartoons of R.K. Laxman,
Takes flight only to get stuck in the bushes.
A gust of wind can change the profile of these characters
They can return with a change in apparel.

The fog stays for long in February
In February the frost sets in.

नीम राना

ब्लॉक्स को गर, नीचे ऊपर रख के उनको
ऊंची नीची सीढ़ियों से जोड़ दें तो
'नीम राना' का क़िला बनता है उनसे

थोड़ी थोड़ी सीढ़ीयां चुगती उचकती फ़ाख़्ताओं की तरह हैं
नीचे ऊपर को फुदकती रहती हैं सब
तंग गलयारे, मिलाते जोड़ते हैं आंगनों को

राना जब ज़िंदा थे और रहते थे इस में
यूं खड़े रहते थे चाकर नीचे ऊपर
ढाल और तलवारें लेकर
जिस तरह शतरंज के ख़ानों में मोहरे
राना जब आवाज़ देते, या उन्हें रानी बुलाती
मोहरे अपने आप चल कर दूसरे ख़ाने में हुक़्क़े की तरह सीधे
खड़े हो जाया करते थे
मुंतज़िर रहते थे अगला कश लगे तो 'लाट' निकले
फिर से कोई हुकुम जारी हो
दो रुखी तोपें क़िले पर
जैसे दो मूंछों को ताव दे के राना ने
बस्तियों के रुख़ पे रखा है!

Neemrana

If building blocks are arranged one upon another
And then joined by steps going up and down
The fort of Neemrana emerges.

A few steps, here and there, are like doves frolicking
    about
Up and down they prance around
As narrow alleyways join and divide courtyards.

When the Rana was alive and lived here
Minions stood everywhere
With shields and swords
Like pieces on a chessboard
When the Rana called out, or was called by his Rani,
The pieces would move on their own to another square
Standing erect like hookahs
They used to wait for the next puff
And the next command
Like the Rana's freshly twirled moustache.

बड़ा दिलचस्प है इन ब्लॉक्स में इतिहास भर के,
उसके ग़लीचों पे अपने पांव रखना, और चलना
    उसकी मच्छर–दानियों में लेट जाना
रोज़ मूंद आंखों में बोझल ख़्वाब भरना

अब क़िला ओढ़े हुए ये एक होटल है
रक़्स–गह जो देर तक रोशन रहा करती थी पहले
अब डिनर के वक़्त अक्सर हम वहां पर,
मेज़ों पर शम्एं जला कर
ठुमरियों के टेप सुनते हैं
और पतिंगे नाचते हैं!!

There were two cannons on the fort
Dominating the populace below
To infuse these blocks with the past is a fascinating
   exercise
To walk on its narrow alleyways and saunter along
To lie back under the mosquito nets
And fill one's closed eyes with fading dreams.

Now the fort is wrapped around a hotel
The dancing halls that earlier glowed till late in the night
Is where, often, at dinner
Sitting at candlelit tables
We listen to thumris played on tapes
While moths dance around!

कभी कभी यूं भी होता है ऊंचे पहाड़ों पर

कभी कभी यूं भी होता है ऊंचे पहाड़ों पर
चांद निकल कर देखता है अब कितनी बर्फ़ गिरी है
मौसम ठीक लगे तो एक एक कर के तारों को बुलवाता है
कुछ ऊन पहन कर आते हैं, कुछ कुछ कांपते कांपते,
    उसकी आंख से ओझल होकर छुप भी जाते हैं!

आधी रात होते होते जब आसमान भर जाता है
''हुश हुश'' की आवाज़ें आने लगती हैं
और गड़रिया हांक के ले जाता है अपने तारों को!

Sometimes, High on the Mountains .

Sometimes, high on the mountains, it so happens
The moon comes out to see how much snow has fallen
And, if the weather is calm, calls the stars, one by one
Some come all dressed in woollens, others shivering
And some hide, escaping his eye.

As midnight approaches and the sky is star-laden
Voices of 'hoosh, hoosh' begin to resound
And the shepherd takes his flock of stars away!

पहाड़ों से बिछड़ के लौटता हूं तो . . .!

पहाड़ों से बिछड़ के लौटता हूं तो
कई दिन तक उतरता रहता हूं उनसे,
ख़ला में लटका रहता हूं
कहीं पांव नहीं पड़ते!

बहुत से आस्मां बांहों में भर जाता है
                        वो नीचे नहीं आता
हवाएं फूल जाती हैं, पकड़ के पसलियां मेरी
कभी रातें उठा लेती हैं बग़लों से
कभी दिन ठेल देते हैं हवा में . . .
कई दिन तक मेरे पांव नहीं लगते ज़मीं से!!

When I Return from the Mountains

When I have to part from the mountains
It takes me many days to descend
I remain hung in the space
My feet are unable to touch the ground.

A lot of sky nestles in my arms
The winds puff up, holding me by my ribs
Sometimes the nights lift me from the side
Sometimes the days push me into the breeze
For many days my feet do not touch the ground.

आदतन . . .

आदतन . . .
झूठ बोलता है 'रेन ट्री'
सर पे खुश्क आसमान है मगर
उसके नीचे की ज़मीन, भीगी रहती है!

गुज़र चुका है मौसमे बहार भी
ख़िज़ां गिराती फिर रही है पत्ते दौड़ दौड़ कर
और ये, कैसे इत्मीनान से
रंग में डुबो डुबो के
फूल रख रहा है शाख़ शाख़ पर
इस की शायराना आदतों का कोई क्या करे
आदतन . . . झूठ बोलता है 'रेन ट्री'!!

Habit

By habit
The rain tree tells lies:
Above its head the sky is dry
But the ground below is drenched.

The season of spring is long over
Autumn scurries around wrenching down leaves
But this tree, with amazing equanimity
Dips flowers deep in colour
And places them on branch after branch.

What can anyone do with such poetic traits?
The rain tree tells lies . . . by habit!

कितना लंबा होगा झरना

कितना लंबा होगा झरना
सारा दिन कोहसार पकड़ के नीचे उतरता रहता है
फिर भी ख़त्म नहीं होता . . .!

सारा दिन ही बादलों में, ये वादी चलती रहती है
न रुकती है, न थमती है
बारिश का बर्बत भी बजता रहता है
लंबी लंबी हवा की उंगलियां थकतीं नहीं
जंगल में आवाज़ नदी की
बोलते बोलते बैठ गई है
भारी लगती है आवाज़ नदी की!!

How Long Must Be This Stream

How long must be this stream
That, holding on to the rock,
It can keep descending the whole day
Without ever stopping!

This valley journeys the whole day in the clouds
It neither stops nor pauses
The harp of rain keeps playing
The long fingers of the wind never tire
In the forest, the river's voice
Has become hoarse by constantly talking
It is heavy and gruff, the river's voice!

दिसंबर

दिसंबर में हमेशा बर्फ़ पड़ती है
दिसंबर लग गया है

दरख़्तों को पता है, पंछियों को लौट कर आने में
लंबा वक़्त जाएगा
गड़रिए ख़ाली कर जाएंगे सारी वादियां और
हांक कर ले जाएंगे भेड़ों के रेवड़
ढलानों से उतर जाएंगे सब
सूरज गुरूब होने से पहले
बड़े सूने लगेंगे शाम के जंगल
बिना आहट उतर आएंगी बर्फ़ें
दिसंबर लग गया है

कई फ़ुट बर्फ़ के नीचे भी लेकिन घास अपने
बीज लेकर ज़िंदा रहती है
कि जैसे दर्द अपनी कांगड़ी लेकर मेरे सीने में
सांसें लेता रहता है!!

December

In December it always snows
And December has begun!

The trees know the birds will take long
To return;
The shepherds will leave the valleys empty
Round up their sheep
And descend down the slopes
Before the sun sets;
The forests at dusk will look so forlorn
And without the slightest sound
The snow will come down;
December has begun.

But several feet below the snow
The grass with its seeds stays alive
Just like pain, with its burning embers,
Breathes on, deep inside my heart!

Gulzar

नए नए ही चांद पे रहने आए थे

नए नए ही चांद पे रहने आए थे
हवा न पानी, गर्द, न कूड़ा
न कोई आवाज़, न हरकत
ग्रेविटी बिन तो पांव नहीं पड़ते हैं कहीं
अपने वज़न का भी अहसास नहीं होता!

चलते हैं
जो भी घुटन है, जैसी भी हो
चल के ज़मीं पर रहते हैं!!

New on the Moon

We were the new settlers come to stay on the moon
No breeze, no water, no dust, no garbage
Nor any sound or movement
Without gravity, even our feet could not find the ground
We could not even feel how much we weighed!

Let us go back now
Whatever the suffocation, however bad it is,
The earth is where we'll stay!

धूप की उंगलियां जब शाख़ों से छन कर

धूप की उंगलियां जब शाख़ों से छन कर
पेड़ की जांघों को सहलाती हैं झुक कर
मैंने देखा है उन्हें शर्म से नम, और शिकायत करते
लोग बदफ़ालियां भी करते हैं, और . . .
नाम लिख जाते हैं चाकू से मेरी जांघों पर!

भ, च, बाज़ नहीं आते उन्हें लाख कहें!!

The Fingers of the Sun

When the fingers of the sun
Come through the branches
And bend down to caress the thighs of the tree
I have seen the tree become numb with shame, and
    complain:
People do bad things on me, and—
Gouge out their names with knives on my thighs!

Alas! No reprimand can ever make these people change
    their ways!

बाल पकड़ के सीधा खड़ा करता है पेड़ को सूरज

बाल पकड़ के सीधा खड़ा करता है पेड़ को सूरज लेकिन
लेकिन वो . . . मिट्टी की गोद से उठने को तैयार नहीं होता
हाथ पांव पटकता है
स्कूल में जाने से डरता है
'रैगिंग' होगी

आते जाते हवा थपेड़े देगी
चिड़ियां चोंच से मारेंगी
कोई अगर . . . कंधों पर आ बैठे तो कौन उड़ाएगा?

सूरज लेकिन खींचता रहता है बालों से
पेड़ कर ये मिट्टी की ममता जाती नहीं
जितना बड़ा होता है,
उतना ही गहरा मिट्टी में और उतरता रहता है!

When the Sun Pulls the Tree Up by Its Hair

Catching the tree by its hair
The sun makes it stand straight
But the tree throws a tantrum:
It is afraid to go to school
Where ragging takes place!

The wind, every time it passes, will push me around,
    it says,
Birds will peck at me
If one sits on my shoulders
Who will make it fly away?

But as the sun keeps pulling it by the hair
The tree cannot forsake the motherly pull of the earth
The taller it grows
The deeper it descends into the earth.

इतनी छोटी दुबली पतली सी पगडंडी

इतनी छोटी दुबली पतली सी पगडंडी
रोज़ पहाड़ की चोटी पर चढ़ जाती है!
और इतनी चौड़ी तारकोल की पक्की सड़क है
कितने बल खाती है लेकिन
ऊपर तक वो जा नहीं सकती!!

Such a Small Pathway

Such a small, lean and thin pathway
Climbs all the way to the mountain's pinnacle!
And such a wide, metalled road
Cannot reach the top
No matter how many loops it takes!

बुलंद क़द है, ऊंची भूरे रंग की चट्टान चंबा में

बुलंद क़द है, ऊंची भूरे रंग की चट्टान चंबा में
और उसके बीचों बीच इक शगाफ़ बहता है!
महीन धार से बुना हुआ है एक झरना पानी का
हमेश ही से देखता हूं
इस का ये 'इज़ारबंद' लटकता रहता है!!

The Rock in Chamba

It stands tall and mighty, this tan-coloured rock in
    Chamba
And from its very centre a stream flows
Falling like a spring woven by a slender thread
I have seen it always
Its pyjama cord hanging out in the open!

कैरला

तुम्हारे 'बैक वाटर्ज़' कैरला—पानी के गांव हैं!
वहां के पेड़, बाशिंदे वहां के
वहां सब्ज़े की गलियां हैं
समंदर जब भी अपनी उंगलियों से बाल सहलाता है सब्ज़े के
ज़मीं पर सुरसुरी सी दौड़ जाती है
तुम्हारे नारियल के पेड़ मीलों दूर तक हंसते हैं
                        उनको गुदगुदी महसूस होती है!

कभी देखा है, जब 'बहरे—अरब' के पेट में बल पड़ने लगते हैं
वो घुंघराले घने बादल उड़ाता है
हवाएं बादलों के गुच्छे लेकर दौड़ जाती हैं
जुनूबी हिंद पूरा भीग जाता है
कभी नक़्शे में देखो तो . . .

तुम्हारे 'बैक वाटर्ज़' कैरला, लगता है ज़ुल्फ़ें हैं समंदर की
हमेशा उड़ती रहती हैं
समंदर लहरों में कंघी नहीं करते!

Kerala

Kerala, your backwaters are like villages of water!
The trees there are the real inhabitants
And the alleyways are made of grassy undergrowth.
Whenever the sea caresses the green grass with its fingers
A quiver runs through the earth
Your coconut trees feel a tickling sensation
And can be seen laughing for miles around!

Have you ever seen, when the gut of the Arabian Sea
      begins to churn,
How it sets into flight coiled, dense clouds?
The wind runs off with these bunches of clouds
And all of South India is drenched.
Sometimes, look at a map . . .

Your backwaters, Kerala, look like the curls of the sea
Always flying in the breeze
The sea does not comb the hair of its waves!

बेल्जियन क्रिस्टली बर्तन

बेल्जियन क्रिस्टली बर्तन
बिना तरतीब के रक्खे बादल
प्लेन जब इनसे गुज़रता है तो लगता है अभी
टूटेगा बर्तन कोई!
कांच गिरने की ज़मीं पर अभी आवाज़ भी होगी!
है ना!!

Belgian Crystal

Clouds, placed randomly,
Look like Belgian crystal
When the plane passes through them
It seems they'll break any moment
And you'll hear the imminent sound of broken glass
Hitting the ground!
Isn't it?

पत्थर पे पत्थर रख रख के

पत्थर पे पत्थर रख रख के
एक मकां ऊपर उठने की कोशिश में है
साथ की छत पे कुहनी रख के
आसमान का कोई कोना देख सके!

और इक बिल्डिंग,
सामने डट के खड़ी हुई है
उसकी पीठ से पीठ लगा के एक इमारत
उठने की कोशिश में, घुटनों पर बैठी है
'स्टील' के 'गर्डर' पहन रही है
बाएं तरफ़ की बिल्डिंग का क़द
उसके क़द से ऊंचा नहीं पर
उस से परली छत पे कुछ मीनार खड़े हैं
चिम्नियों जैसे लगते हैं
कोई 'होर्डिंग' दमक चमक करती रहती है

नीचे देखो तो कारें ही कारें हैं
लोग इक दूसरे के पैरों पर पांव रखके
कूद फलांग के चलते हैं
दो बालिश्त का ख़ाली वक़्फ़ा ही मिल जाए पास कहीं
पूरी पलकें खोल के देखें, इतनी सी तो जगह मिले!
आसमान का कोई कोना देख सके!
एक मकां ऊपर उठने की कोशिश में है!!

Placing Stone Upon Stone

Placing stone upon stone
A house is trying to raise itself
Placing its elbow on the neighbouring roof
It strains to see a corner of the sky!

Another building
Stands stoutly in front;
Cheek by jowl with it, a structure
Sits crouched on its knees
Seeking to get up
By wearing steel girders;
To the left, a building
Is smaller in height
But on the roof beyond are some minarets
Chimneys perhaps
While a hoarding dazzles with its array of lights.

People, with feet on other people's feet,
Hop and skip about.

If only a two-yard empty space could be found nearby
A tiny gap, from where, with its eyes fully open
It can see a corner of the sky!
A house is trying to raise itself!

शहर की सारी फ़िज़ा मैली है

शहर की सारी फ़िज़ा मैली है
घाम और पित से घिस कर चलना पड़ता है
'लारवे' मर जाते हैं ख़ालिस पानी में
साफ़ हवा में खांसने लगते हैं अब लोग!

धूल और मिट्टी से अब फ़र्क़ नहीं पड़ता
चुटकी से झड़ जाती हैं
साबुन की इक चिकनी चक्की काफ़ी है अब
कपड़े और किरदार सफ़ा रखने के लिए!!

The Dirty City

The atmosphere of the whole city is dirty
We slither around in the prickly heat
Larvae die in clean water
And people begin to cough when the air is pure!

Dust and grime makes no difference now
They can be brushed away easily
An ordinary cake of soap is enough
To keep one's clothes and character clean!

इन जंगली पौधों के डंठल पर . . .

इन जंगली पौधों के डंठल पर . . .
कुछ लफ़्ज़ निकल आते हैं कभी,
पर नज़्म नहीं फलती कोई . . .!

इन पौधों को खुराक नहीं मिलती कि जड़ें
मिट्टी को पकड़ के बैठ सकें
इन पौधों को गमले भी नहीं मिलते कि जड़ें महफ़ूज़ रहें . . .
सड़कों पे फेंक दिए जाते हैं
धूल, भूख, और भीक में पलते रहते हैं
और उनमें कहीं, कोई कोई
ठोकर खाकर जा गिरता है बहती नाली के कीचड़ में
वो मिट्टी पानी पाकर उगने लगता है . . .!

फिर और सड़क
एक और नई ठोकर
एक और दलित पौदा!!

Dalit Plant

On the branches of these wild plants
Some words occasionally sprout
But never a full poem.

These plants never have enough nutrients
To allow their roots to grasp the soil
They do not get pots where their roots can be nurtured
They are thrown on the roads
And survive in the dust, and in hunger and charity
Some few among them, sometimes,
Get kicked into the slime of a flowing gutter
And finding water and soil they begin to grow . . .

Another road, again
Another kick—
And another Dalit plant!

कुआं बंद हो रहा था

कुआं बंद हो रहा था
कुएं की सांस घुटती जा रही थी
मनों मिट्टी गिराई जा चुकी थी,
बहुत से तख़्ते काटे जा रहे थे

सलाख़ें रख के दो जानिब
पुराना मिस्त्री तसले में सीमेंट घोल कर फैला रहा था
कुआं बंद हो रहा था . . .

परों को फड़फड़ा कर उसके पानी में नहाती थी
परेशां थी . . .
बड़ी बेचैन थी पीपल पे उड़ती फ़ाख़्ता दिन भर
परेशां थी कि, इक ज़िंदा कुएं को लोग क्यों दफ़ना रहे थे!!

The Burial of a Well

A well was being closed
Slowly, it was asphyxiating
Tons of earth had been poured in
And many planks were being cut.

With iron rods placed across
An old mason, mixing cement in a pan, was spreading
      it around
The well was being closed.

She used to flutter her wings and have a bath in its waters
She was worried
Flying about the peepul tree the whole day
The dove was deeply restless
Vexed about why people were burying a living well!

कुएं के आस पास अब कुछ नहीं है

कुएं के आस पास अब कुछ नहीं है
ज़रा से फ़ासले पर इक पुराना पेड़ जामुन का
अब उस पर फल नहीं आते . . .
मगर कुछ फुंदने पत्तों के लग कर, सूख जाते हैं
कुआं भी अब अतरने लग गया है
कुएं की सब मुंडेरें ढह चुकी हैं
हरी काई है, दीवारों पे काली पड़ रही है
कोई आता नहीं गांव की पगडंडी से पानी खींचने अब!
डुबोए कल्सी पानी में, उठाए, फिर डुबोए
कुएं में झांक कर कुछ गुनगुनाए
या अपने अक्स ही से बात करले!

वो कह के तो गई थी, फिर से लौटेगी
मैं छोड़े कुएं की मानिंद वहीं ठहरा हुआ हूं
उतरने लग गया हूं
खुष्क होता जा रहा हूं!

The Abandoned Well

Now, nothing is left around the well
Just a jamun tree, a little distance away,
That no longer fruits.
A few leaves occasionally grow, only to die
Even the water in the well has begun to ebb
The retaining walls of the well have crumbled
Green slime and blackened walls are all that remain
Nobody comes down the village's pathway to draw
    water any more,
To dip the bucket in the water, pull it up, dip it again
Peep down and hum something
Or just talk to one's reflection!

When she left she did say she would return
Like the abandoned well, I wait
Beginning to ebb
Shrivelling by the day.

दाग़दार, चितकबरी सुबह निकली है

दाग़दार, चितकबरी सुबह निकली है
आकाश पे सिलवटें दिखती हैं
सियाह चिकत्ते पंजे मार के बैठे हैं!

चादर के ऊपर से जैसे
गीले गीले पंजे लेकर
रात की काली बिल्ली कूद के निकली है!

Stained Dawn

Spotted, this dawn is stained,
The creases on the sky are visible
Black-and-white paw-marks all over.

As though, over the sheet,
With dripping paws,
The night's black cat has sprinted across!

आंख मिचोली

छोटा सा शीशे का टुकड़ा
घास के अंदर छुप के बैठा
मेरी आंख पे सूरज मार के खुश होता है, हंसता है

सूरज खुश है,
छोटा सा शीशे का टुकड़ा
घास में रख के खेल रहा है
मेरी आंख पे छींटे मार के छेड़ रहा है

आंख पे एक हथेली रख के
मैं फ़ौरन दोनों की आंखों से ओझल हो जाता हूं
उंगलियों की झिर्रियों से वो दोनों झांक के
                        मुझको ढूंढ़ने लगते हैं
और मैं आंखें बंद किए
तेरी गोद में सर रख के छुप जाता हूं!
कायनात से आंख मिचोली खेल रहा हूं!!

Hide-and-Seek

A small piece of glass
Hiding in the grass
Laughs in delight as it reflects the sun on to my eyes.

The sun is happy
That by using a small piece of glass
Placed in the grass
It can tease me by spraying my eyes with light.

Covering my eyes with one palm
I disappear from both their sights
They peer through my fingers to find me
And I, with my eyes closed,
Put my head in your lap to hide.
I am playing hide-and-seek with the universe.

दरयाये मांडवी

समंदर है या दरया है?
अगर दरया है तो कितना वसी है
कहीं कोई किनारा ही नज़र आता नहीं है
समन्द्र है तो जाने कितने दरयाओं का संगम है
जहां भर के सभी दरया इसी में आके गिरते हैं,
मगर फिर भी . . .
समंदर से कोई दरया नहीं बह कर निकलता!

समंदर है तो फिर तू क्या समंदर है?
सभी तुझ में तो आते हैं
कोई तुझ से नहीं आता!!

River Mandavi

Is it a river or an ocean?
If a river, then how wide is it
That the shores are not visible?
If an ocean, then of how many rivers is it the confluence?
All the rivers falling brimful into it
And yet
No river flows out of the ocean!

If an ocean, what kind of ocean are you?
After all, everyone flows into you
But no one flows out from you!

खुलने लगे हैं आसमान के सिरे उफ़क़ से

खुलने लगे हैं आसमान के सिरे उफ़क़ से
कितनी जगह से अब ये ख़ैमा उधड़ रहा है
सारा दिन बैठा नज़्मों के टांके लगा कर
उस को रफ़ू करता रहता हूं!

The Sky

The seams of the sky have begun to separate from the
    firmament
This tent is now coming apart in so many places
Using the stitches of my poetry
I spend my whole day darning!

ज़मीं को जादू आता है!

मेरे इस बाग़ की मिट्टी में कुछ तो है
ये जादुई ज़मीं है क्या?
ज़मीं को जादू आता है!

अगर अमरूद बीजूं मैं, तो ये अमरूद देती है
अगर जामुन की गुटली डालूं तो जामुन भी देती है
करेला तो करेला . . . नींबू तो नींबू!

अगर मैं फूल मांगूं तो गुलाबी फूल देती है
मैं जो रंग दूं उसे, वो रंग देती है
ये सारे रंग क्या उसने कहीं नीचे छुपा रखे हैं मिट्टी में?
बहुत खोदा मगर कुछ भी नहीं निकला . . .!
ज़मीं को जादू आता है!

ज़मीं को जादू आता है
बड़े करतब दिखाती है
ये लंबे लंबे ऊंचे ताड़ के जब पेड़, उंगली पर उठाती है
तो गिरने भी नहीं देती!
हवाएं खूब हिलाती हैं, ज़मीं हिलने नहीं देती!

The Magical Earth

There is something indeed in the earth of my garden
Is this earth magical?
The earth knows how to do magic!

If I sow a guava seed, it gives me guavas
If I put in a jamun kernel it gives me jamuns
A bitter gourd for a bitter gourd, a lemon for a lemon!

If I ask for a flower, it gives me pink flowers
Whatever colour I give to it, it returns that to me
Has it hidden all these colours in the soil below?
I dug a lot but found nothing
The earth knows how to do magic!

The earth knows how to do magic
It shows so many tricks
When it balances these long coconut trees on its fingers
It does not even let them fall!
The wind does its best, but the earth does not let them
     fumble!

मेरे हाथों से शर्बत, दूध, पानी
कुछ गिरे सब डीक जाती है
ये कितना पानी पीती है!
ग़टक जाती है जितना दो,
इसे लोटे से दो या बाल्टी से,
या नल दिन भर खुला रख दो
अजब ;ग़ज़बद्ध है, पेट भरता ही नहीं इस का
सुना है ये नदी को भी छुपा लेती है अंदर!
ज़मीं को जादू आता है!!

ज़मीं के नीचे क्या 'चीनी' की खानें हैं?
खटाई की चटानें हैं?
फलों में मीठा कैसे डालती है ये ज़मीं?
                          लाती कहां से है?

अनारों, बैरों और आमों में, सेबों में,
सभी मीठों में भी मीठे अलग हैं,
कि पत्ते खाओ तो फीके हैं और फल मीठे लगते हैं
मौसंबी मीठी है तो नींबू खट्टा है!
यक़ीनन जादू आता है!!
वगर न बांस फीका, सख़्त, और गन्नों में रस क्यों है?

ज़मीं के पेट में क्या कोई मक़नातीस का टुकड़ा रक्खा है,
कि जो गिरता है, उसके पास जाता है
वो चिड़िया हो या 'उल्का' हो!
ज़मीं को जादू आता है!!

A sherbet, or milk, or water
Anything may fall, it absorbs them all
How much water does it drink?!
It gulps down whatever you give
Be it from a jug or a bucket
Amazingly, its stomach never fills
I have heard that it can even hide a river inside!
The earth knows how to do magic!

Are there sugar godowns under the earth?
Or rocks of lime?
How does this earth put sweetness into fruits?
From where does it get all this?

Pomegranates, plums and mangoes—in all of them
Sweetness, but of different kinds
The leaves tasteless but the fruits sweet
The musambi sweet, the lemon sour
Undoubtedly, it knows magic!
Otherwise, why is the bamboo tasteless, and the
    sugarcane sweet?

कल इक पहाड़ पे सर रखके सो रहा था जब

कल इक पहाड़ पे सर रखके सो रहा था जब
मैं आस्मान की आहट से उठ के बैठ गया
बड़े क़रीब से गुज़रा था आस्मां कल भी
ख़ज़ाना लूट के लाया था कायनात से वो
न जाने कितने सितारे थे, कितने सय्यारे
मैं उसको जाता हुआ देखता रहा षब भर
फिर इक जगह पे रुका—
उफ़क़ पे पांव रखा बोला 'खुल सिम सिम!'
इक आफ़ताब की चट्टान हटते हटते हटी,
तो दिन का ग़ार खुला
वो ख़ज़ाना देखकर चुंधिया गईं आंखें
मैं इक ग़रीब, अली बाबा, और मेरा गधा
बताओ कितना उठा लेंगे, गर उठा भी लें!!

The Mountain and the Sky

Yesterday as I slept with my head on a mountain
I was woken up by a movement in the sky
Yesterday too it passed very close by
Having plundered a fortune from the cosmos
Stars beyond count, infinite galaxies
I kept watching the whole night as it journeyed
And then it stopped
Putting one leg on the horizon it said: 'Open Sesame!'
The rock of the sun moved grudgingly
And the cave opened
Watching that fortune my eyes glazed over
I, but a poor Ali Baba with my donkey,
How much, pray tell me, could I take, even if I could!

टहनी पर बैठा था वो

टहनी पर बैठा था वो
नीचे तालाब था पानी का और,
तालाब के अंदर आसमान था
डूबने से डर लगता था
न तैरा, न उड़ा, न डूबा
टहनी पर ही बैठे बैठे बिलाख़िर वो सूख गया!
एक अकेला शाख़ का पत्ता!

One Lone Leaf

It was perched on a branch
Below were the waters of a lake,
And underneath lay the sky.
It was afraid of being drowned
But . . .
It neither swam, nor drowned, nor flew away
It just sat on the branch, and finally wilted
One lone leaf on a branch!

ये सब जो सैर को सुबह निकलते हैं

ये सब जो सैर को सुबह निकलते हैं
ये सब फुटबॉल लगते हैं
बड़े, छोटे, मचकते, फूलते, सिलते, उधड़ते,
उछलते और लुढ़कते बॉल सारे
अकेले खेलती है ज़िंदगी इनसे
भगाती है, गिराती है, उठा के कॉर्नर से किक लगाती है
कि जो भी गोल में जाए,
वो फिर वापस नहीं आता!!

The Walkers

All these people who stir out for a walk in the morning
Look like footballs:
Big, small, twirling, puffed, patched, opening at the seams,
Jumping, swaying footballs!
Life plays with them
Makes them run, fall, or picks them up, only to kick
    them from a corner!
Whoever enters the goalpost
Never returns!

'लेवी शोमेकर'

अब तो आदत सी हो गई है मुझे,
रास्ता पार करने से पहले . . .
इक नज़र आसमां की तरफ़, सर उठा के देख लेता हूं।
मार्ज़, मर्कुरी, वीनस
जलते बुझते अमीर ज़ादे सभी,
दौड़ते रहते हैं ख़लाओं में . . .
पिछले हफ्ते ही 'जुपिटर' के सीने पर
अंधा धुंद जाके टकराया।
अपने ही शहर का कोई,
'लेवी शोमेकर' के नाम का कोमेट!

सैकड़ों मीलों तक उड़े शोले,
कितनी सदियां लगेंगी, सोचो तो,
'जुपिटर' के वो दाग़ भरने में!

Levi Schumaker

Now it has become a habit with me:
Before crossing a road
I glance at the sky, lift my head to see it!
Mars, Mercury, Venus
Blazing, fading, filthy rich all of them
Running about perpetually in space!
Just last week, a comet from our own vicinity
Went and blindly crashed into the chest of Jupiter
Its name was Levi Schumaker.

Burning embers flew about for miles
Just think, how long it will take
For the scabs on Jupiter to heal!

A comet Levi Schumaker crashed on the planet Jupiter in July
1994.

मीर' से नज़ारा

एयरपोर्ट के रनवे, पर फैली पसरी ये रात बहुत अच्छी लगती है
दूर तलक फैला अंधेरा, कायनात का लगता है
नीले पीले लाल बल्ब सब . . .
दूर दूर तक
जैसे दूसरे सय्यारे हैं, जाग रहे हैं
लगता है मैं
स्पेस के 'मीर' स्टेशन पर आकर बैठा हूं
और किसी दुनिया के सफ़र पे जाना है
प्लैनेट, ए.के. चार सौ अड़तीस!

भारी भरकम एक परिंदा
ख़ला से आके आधी रात उतरता है
रोबो जैसे लोग निकलते हैं पंखों से
और भंवराती रात में गुम हो जाते हैं
कई तरह की आंधियों की आवाज़ें करता
अफ़लाकी परिंदा उड़ जाता है
कायनात के अंधेरे में फिर से गुम हो जाता है
पारे जैसी ख़ामोशी रह जाती है
ठंडे लिक वडा अंधेरे पर रखी रात
हिलते हिलते थोड़ी देर में थम जाती है
एयरपोर्ट के 'रनवे' पर फैली पसरी ये रात
                              बहुत अच्छी लगती है!!

View from Mir

This night, sprawling, spread out, on the airport tarmac
Is so bewitching
Stretching out in the distance the darkness appears to be
Of the cosmos
The myriads of blue, yellow, red bulbs
Glimmering far into the horizon
Look like separate galaxies, wide awake
It seems as if I am sitting in the space station Mir
Ready for a voyage to another world . . .
Planet AK-438!

A large and heavy bird
Descends at midnight
Robot-like figures emerge from its wings
And disappear in the swirling night;
With the sound of several storms
The heavenly bird flies away
And is again lost in the engulfing darkness of the universe
A fragile silence is all that is left
The quivering night, placed on liquid darkness, slowly
        settles;
This night, sprawling, spread out, on the airport tarmac
Is so bewitching!

छुट्टी के दिन . . .!

छुट्टी के दिन . . .
सत्य पॉल आनंद और मैं
'कॉस्मोस' जेबों में भर कर
अक्सर चांद के पीछे वाले आस्मान में जाकर खेला करते हैं

सात सितारे ऊपर के,
दो नीचे रख के
नौ पत्थर का पिट्टू खेलना
'किरमिच' वाली चांद की गेंद की उतार के ले जाया करते हैं

कभी कभी अंटी होती है
ये वीनस का कंचा है
और वो जुपिटर का बंटा!

गिल्ली डंडा भी जमता है
चल कोमेट का डंडा लेकर
'शूमेकर' की गिल्ली से
गिल्ली डंडा खेलेंगे!

इत्ती ज़ोर न मारियो गिल्ली
कांच ज़मीं का टूट गया तो
फ़िश टैंक की सारी मच्छियां स्पेस में गिर के मर जाएंगी
और बड़े मियां से डांट पड़ेगी!!

The Cosmic Game

During the holidays
Satyapal Anand and I
Would often fill our pockets with the cosmos
And go to the sky behind the moon to play.

With seven stars above
And two placed below
We played *piththu*
With the moon as our canvas ball.

Sometimes we would play marbles,
One lovely Venus
And the other natty Jupiter!

We also played *gilli-danda*:
A comet became our stick
To smack the wooden pellet of 'Schumaker'!

But do not hit so hard
That the earth's glass shatters
For then, all the fish in the fish tank will
Fall in space and die
And then the Old Man will scold us!

Satyapal Anand is a celebrated Urdu poet. We share a love for
the cosmos.

बादल–1

रात को फिर बादल ने आकर
गीले गीले पंजों से जब दरवाज़े पर दस्तक दी
झट से उठ के बैठ गया मैं बिस्तर में

अक्सर नीचे आकर ये कच्ची बस्ती में
लोगों पर गुर्राता है–
लोग बिचारे 'डामर' लेप के दीवारों पर
बंद कर लेते हैं झिरियां
ताकि झांक न पाए घर के अंदर
लेकिन फिर भी–
गुर्राता चिंघाड़ता बादल
अक्सर ऐसे लूट के ले जाता है बस्ती
जैसे ठाकुर का कोई गुंडा
बदमस्ती करता निकले इस बस्ती से!!

The Cloud–1

At night, when the cloud once again
Knocked on my door with its dripping paws,
I woke up immediately and sat up in bed.

It comes down often to this poor settlement
To growl at people;
The helpless folk use tar to seal their walls
So that it is not able to peep inside,
But, even so,
This snarling, shrieking cloud
Often plunders the hamlet
Like some henchman of a feudal lord
Would misbehave passing tipsily through the village!

Gulzar

बादल–2

कल सुबह जब बारिश ने आकर खिड़की पर दस्तक दी थी
नींद में था मैं बाहर अभी अंधेरा था
ये तो कोई वक़्त नहीं था, उठ कर उससे मिलने का
मैंने परदा खींच दिया
गीला गीला एक हवा का झोंका उसने
फूंका मेरे मुंह पर लेकिन
मेरी 'सैंस–ऑफ़–ह्युमर' भी कुछ नींद में थी
मैंने उठ कर ज़ोर से खिड़की के पट उस पर भिड़ दिए
और करवट लेकर, फिर बिस्तर में डूब गया।

शायद बुरा लगा था उसको
गुस्से में खिड़की के कांच पे हथड़ मार के लौट गई वो
दोबारा फिर आई नहीं
खिड़की पर वो चटख़ा कांच अभी बाक़ी है!!

The Cloud–2

Yesterday morning when the rains came and knocked
    on my window
I was still asleep and outside it was dark
This was no time to get up and meet with the rain.
I drew the curtains
But it still blew on my face
A moist, wet breeze
My sense of humour was quite drowsy
I got up and banged the shutters on its face
And, turning my back, sank deep into bed.

Perhaps it felt offended
In anger, it slammed the glass of my window
And never returned.
The cracked glass on the window still remains!

क्लोज़अप!

सर सब्ज़ हरा चेहरा उसका,
दो रोज़ से पीला है
छू जाए हवा का झोंका तो वो कांपने लगता है!

जिस पेड़ पे लटका है,
वो आधा डूब चुका है अब सैलाब के पानी में
कितना पानी और चढ़ेगा, पता नहीं!

वो एक अकेला पत्ता,
पेड़ से कहता जाता है
तू डरना मत . . . मैं हूं ना!
तू डरना मत . . . मैं हूं ना!!

Close-Up of a Leaf

Its lush green face
Has paled in the last two days
It begins to tremble if a gust of wind touches it.

The tree from which it hangs
Is half-drowned in the flood waters
No one knows how much higher the water will rise!

That one leaf
Keeps telling the tree:
Don't be afraid, I'm there!
Don't be afraid, I'm there!

कुल्लू वादी

बादलों में कुछ उड़ती हुई भेड़ें नज़र आती हैं
दुंबे दिखते हैं कभी भालु से कुश्ती लड़ते
ढीली सी पगड़ी में इक बुड्ढा मुझे देखके हैरान सा है

कोई गुज़रा है वहां से शायद
धूप में डूबा हुआ ब्रश लेकर
बर्फ़ों पर रंग छिड़कता हुआ—जिस के क़तरे
पेड़ों की शाख़ों पे भी जाके गिरे हैं

दौड़ के आती है बेचैन हवा झाड़ने रंगीन छींटे
ऊंचे, जाटों की तरह सफ़ में खड़े पेड़ हिला देती है
और इक धुंधले से कोहरे में कभी
मोटरें नीचे उतरती हैं पहाड़ों से तो लगता है
चादरें पहने हुए, दो दो सफ़ों में
पादरी शमे जलाए हुए जाते हैं इबादत के लिए

कुल्लू की वादी में हर रोज़ यही होता है
शाम होते ही उतर आता है बादल नीचे
ओढ़नी डाल के मंज़र पे, मनादी करने
आज दिन भर की नुमाईश थी, यहीं ख़त्म हुई!

Kullu Valley

A few sheep seem to be adrift in the clouds
Lambs appear to be wrestling with bears
An old man in a loosely tied turban stares at me,
    perplexed.

Perhaps someone has passed this way
With a brush dipped in sunshine
Sprinkling colour drops on the snow
Some of which have fallen on to the trees below.

Anxiously the wind runs to wipe away the drops of
    colour
Shaking the tall jat-like trees!
And, in the engulfing mist,
The cars coming down from the mountains
Look like priests wrapped in sheets
Going in line
To light a candle for prayer.

In the valley of Kullu this happens every day:
The moment the sun sets, the clouds descend
To draw a curtain over the display
And announce the closure of today's exhibition.

पहाड़ की आग

लाल सुनहरी झिलमिल करती आग को मैंने,
जल्दी–जल्दी दूर पहाड़ी की चोटी पर चढ़ते देखा था

जैसे केसरी रंग दोशाला ओढ़े बन्नो
परली वादी से माही की बोली सुनकर,
नंगे पांव दौड़ी थी–
फिर उस आग को ऊचे–ऊंचे चीड़ के पेड़ों पर
चढ़ते भी देखा था,
तेज़ हवा में देर तलक लहरा लहरा कर,
बर्फ़ से फूटे एक नए चश्मे को पास बुलाती रही,
'आ जा, मेरे लब लग जा, मैं प्यासी हूं–'
बन्नो का परदेसी माही लौट आया था,
गोटे बाली लाल सुनहरी आग के पास ना आया कोई,
पेड़ों से जब उतरी तो बुझते चेहरे पर राख मली थी!!

Mountain Fire

I have seen the red-gold sparkling fire
Scramble up to the peak of the distant mountain.

She had run barefoot
On hearing the voice of her lover across the valley
Like a bride wrapped in a saffron shawl.
Then I also saw that fire climb up the towering fir trees
Swaying for long in the strong winds
It kept calling out to a spring that had just emerged
From the snow:
'Come, come, kiss me, I am thirsty.'
The bride's beloved had returned from his journey
    abroad
No one came close to the gold-bordered, red, glittering
    fire;
When it descended from the trees
Ash was smeared on its dwindling visage.

लैंडस्केप

कोई मेला लगा है पर्बत पर
सब्ज़ा ज़ारों पे चढ़ रहे हैं लोग
टोलियां कुछ रुकी हुई ढलानों पर
दाग़ लगते हैं इक पके फल पर
दूर सिवन उधेड़ती, चढ़ती,
एक पगडंडी बढ़ रही है सब्ज़े पर!

च्युंटियां लग गई हैं इस पहाड़ी को
सब्ज़ अमरूद सड़ रहा है कोई!

Landscape

A carnival is being held on the mountain
People are clambering on the lush green verdure
Some groups have halted on the slopes
A ripe fruit is marked with stains;
In the distance
A narrow walking-strip climbs up through the grass
Tearing its lush seams apart.

This mountain is afflicted by ants
A ripe guava is rotting!

Gulzar

ख़िज़ां दरवाज़े के बाहर खड़ी थी

ख़िज़ां दरवाज़े के बाहर खड़ी थी
अभी पोशाक से पत्ता कोई उधड़ा नहीं था
सुनहरी सुर्ख़ होने लग गए थे ज़र्द पत्ते
सभी के कान 'गौतम बुध' के जैसे लंबे लंबे
बस इक आवाज़ के सब मुंतज़िर थे
'चलो अब छोड़ो शाख़ें,
त्याग दो बंधन
सबा लेकर निजात अब आ रही है!!'

The Coming of Autumn

Autumn stood just outside the door
No leaf had as yet deserted the season's apparel
With yellowing leaves turning to burnished gold
Their ears were stretched long like that of Gautam Buddha
To hear that one call:
'Come, leave those branches
Break your bonds
The wind is coming for your liberation!'

ख़िज़ां झाड़न लिए पत्ते गिराती फिर रही है क्यों दरख़्तों से

ख़िज़ा झाड़न लिए पत्ते गिराती फिर रही है क्यों दएख़्तों से
ख़िज़ां को क्या हुआ है?
वो बौराई हुई फिरती है जैसे पीले पत्तों पर लिखी कोई इबारत है,
मिटाना चाहती है . . .!

उसे डर है
बहार आई तो पढ़ लेगी
इबारत मौसमों की, बेसाबाती की
कोई मौसम हमेशा के लिए रहता नहीं है!!

Autumn–1

With a duster in hand, why is autumn busy mopping
    up the leaves?
What has happened to it?
Crazy, it scurries around
As though there is something written on the yellow leaves
Which it must erase!

It's afraid
That spring, when it comes, will read
The writing of the seasons:
'It's short-lived, it's perishable.'
No season lasts forever!

पतझड़

जब जब पतझड़ में पेड़ों से पीले पीले
पत्ते मेरे लॉन में आकर गिरते हैं
रात को छत पर जाकर मैं
आकाश को तकता रहता हूं

लगता है कमज़ोर सा पीला चांद भी शायद
पीपल के सूखे पत्ते सा
लहराता लहराता मेरे लॉन में आकर उतरेगा!

Autumn–2

Whenever yellowing leaves fall
On my lawn in autumn
I go up to the roof at night
And stare at the sky.

It seems that this pale, yellowing moon
Will, like the shrivelled peepul leaf,
Come rippling down perhaps to settle on my lawn!

दरया से कहा भी था

दरया से कहा भी था
मुश्किल है समंदर तक
बे—टोक सफ़र करना
कुछ लोग कुदालों से
काटेंगे किनारों को
पत्थरीली ज़मीनों पर
कांटों में घसीटेंगे
पकड़ेंगे पहाड़ों पर
फेंकेंगे चटानों से
मैदानों में घेरेंगे

और पेट के पानी को
फेंटेंगे, बिलोएंगे,

नाराज़ फ़लक तुम पर
ओले बरसाएगा
बदख़्वाह कोई मौसम
लहरों से उधेड़ेगा
पहुंचोगे दहाने पर
तो झाग मरी होगी
और जिस्म कटा होगा

I Told the River

I had even told the river:
It is difficult to travel
Unruffled up to the sea;
Some people will
Use spades to cut your banks
They will drag you
Over stony ground and thorny land
Catch you in the mountains
Throw you down from cliffs
Arrest you in the plains!

And churn and whip up
The waters deep inside you.

An angry sky will
Rain hailstones at you
Some wayward season
Will rip open your waves
When you reach your destination
Your fizz will be no more
And your body dismembered.

Gulzar

मुंह ढांप के आख़िर जब
डूबोगे समंदर में
हर चीज़ फ़ना होगी
तब ख़त्म अना होगी!!

With your head covered up
When, at last, you merge with the ocean
All will be perished
No more, then, shall the ego survive!

बुड्ढा दरया—1

मुंह ही मुंह कुछ बुड़ बुड़ करता बहता रहता है ये बुड्ढा दरया
कोई पूछे, तुझको क्या लेना, क्या लोग किनारों पर करते हैं?
तू मत सुन, मत कान लगा उनकी बातों पर
घाट पे लच्छी को गर झूट कहा है साले माधव ने
तुझको क्या लेना लच्छी से, जाए जाके डूब मरे!

यही तो दुख है दरया को
जन्मी थी तो 'आनोल नाल' उसीके हाथ में सौंपी थी,
                                        झोलन दाई ने . . .
उसने ही सागर पहुंचाए थे वो 'लुटेरे'
कल जब पेट नज़र आएगा, डूब मरेगी
और वो लाश भी उसकी ही गुम करनी होगी!
लाश मिली तो गांव वाले लच्छी को बदनाम करेंगे

मुंह ही मुंह कुछ बुड़ बुड़ करता बहता रहता है ये बुड्ढा दरया!

The Aged River–1

Muttering to himself this aged river keeps flowing on.
Someone can ask him: How are you concerned with
What people do on the shore?
You don't have to hear, or try to catch what they are
    saying
If that scoundrel Madhav lied to Lachchi on the ghat
What have you to do with Lachchi, let her drown and
    die!

But this is precisely the river's grief:
When Lachchi was born, Jhoolan, the midwife,
Put her umbilical cord into his hands
And it was carried to the ocean by him.
If, tomorrow, Lachchi's stomach begins to show
She will drown herself;
If the body is found the villagers will disgrace her
So it will be his job to hide her corpse too!

Muttering to himself this aged river keeps flowing on.

बुड्ढा दरया–2

मुंह ही मुंह कुछ बुड़ बुड़ करता बहता रहता है ये बुड्ढा दरया
दिन दोपहरे मैंने उसको ख़र्राटे लेते देखा है
ऐसा चित बहता है दोनों पांव पसारे
पत्थर फेंकें, टांग से खैंचें, बगले आकर चोंचें मारें
टस से मस होता ही नहीं है . . .!

चौंक उठता है जब बारिश की बूंदें आकर चुभती हैं
धीरे धीरे हांपने लग जाता है उसके पेट का पानी
तिल मिल करता रेत पे दोनों बांहें मारने लगता है
बारिश पतली पतली बूंदों से जब उसके पेट में गुदगुद करती है!

The Aged River–2

Muttering to himself this aged river keeps flowing on.
I have seen him snoring in the middle of the day
Oblivious to the world, feet spread out, flowing along;
Nothing—not stones thrown at him
Or his legs pulled, or birds pecking at him
Can make him budge even a bit!

But he wakes up with a start when raindrops prick him
Slowly, his waters begin to gasp
With a shudder he begins to throw his arms about on
    the sand
As the rain's thin, pincer drops tickle his stomach!

बुड्ढा दरया–3

मुंह ही मुंह कुछ बुड़ बुड़ करता बहता रहता है ये बुड्ढा दरया
पेट का पानी धीरे धीरे सूख रहा है
दुबला दुबला रहता है अब
कूद के गिरता था ये जिस पत्थर से पहले
वो पत्थर अब धीरे से लटका के उसको
अगले पत्थर से कहता है
इस बुड्ढे को हाथ पकड़ के पार करा दे!

The Aged River–3

Muttering to himself this aged river keeps flowing on.
His waters within are slowly drying up
Shrunk in size, he looks emaciated
Now, the stone, from which he used to earlier leap down,
Gently suspends him below
And tells the next stone:
Hold this old man's hand and help him across!

बारिश

पानी का पेड़ है बारिश, जो पहाड़ों पे उगा करता है
शाख़ें बहती हैं, उमड़ती हुईं, बल खाती हुईं
बर्फ़ के बीज गिरा करते हैं
झरने पकते तो झुमकों की तरह झूलने लगते है कोहस्तानों पर
बेलें गिरती हैं छतों से
मौसमी पेड़ है मौसम में उगा करता है!

Rain

The rain is a tree of water that grows in the mountains
The branches flow, cascading, rippling forth
Seeds of snow fall
When springs mature they swing like eardrops from
    rocks
Creepers overflow from rooftops
It's a seasonal tree that grows when the season comes!

सीलन

बस एक ही सुर में, एक ही लय पे सुबह से देख—
देख कैसे बरस रहा है उदास पानी
फुहार के मलमली दुपट्टे से उड़ रहे हैं
तमाम मौसम टपक रहा है
पलक पलक रिस रही है ये कायनात सारी
हर एक शय भीग भीग कर देख कैसी बोझल सी हो गई है
दिमाग़ की गीली गीली सोचों से
भीगी भीगी उदास यादें टपक रही हैं

थके थके से बदन में बस धीरे धीरे
सांसों का गर्म लोबान जल रहा है।

Dampness

To just one tune, one beat, since morning
See, the sad waters are raining down;
Raindrops fly about like a *malmali* dupatta
The entire season drips
Moment by moment the whole universe is dripping:
Drenched, every object seems to droop
From the wet, soaked thoughts of the mind
Sodden, sad memories drip.

In this tired, weary body
Only the hot incense of breath burns, slowly.

न्यूक्लियर के बाद

सब से खुबरू था वो सय्यारा नीले रंग का!
कहकशां की आंख था . . .

कहकशां में उड़ते उड़ते,
इक बड़ी 'इनर्जी' ने
छोटी इक इनर्जी से कहाः कुछ इस तरह हुआ . . .

कुछ नहीं था पहले उस ज़मीन पर, आसमान भी नहीं
पानी था, शफ़ाफ़ था,
पानियों पे चलती रहती थी हवा,
गैसों का धुआं था, और कुछ नहीं . . .
रात भी हुआ ही करती थी मगर,
अंधेरा चिकना लगता था, चमकता था,
पानी में भी कहकशां का अक्स देख सकते थे
अपनी कहकशां में तो . . .
सब से खुबरू था वो सय्यारा नीले रंग का!

छोटी उस इनर्जी ने
मुड़ के देखा इक जला हुआ ज़मीं का टुकड़ा घूमता हुआ
गिरने वाला था, किसी भी वक़्त आफ़ताब में
एक बार टिमटा के फिर कहा इनर्जी ने,
और फिर ज़मीन को . . .
जाने कैसे लग गई थी ज़िंदगी!
धीरे धीरे . . .
उस ज़मीं को खा गई . . . ज़िंदगी!!

After the Nuclear . . .

The most beautiful was that blue-coloured planet
It was the very eye of the galaxy.

Adrift among the galaxies
A bigger energy addressed a smaller one:
'It happened somewhat like this . . .'

There was absolutely nothing on that earth, not even
     the sky
Only water and transparent light
The winds blew incessantly over the waters
There were gas clouds, and nothing else
The night did fall but
The darkness looked glossy, it gleamed
One could see the galaxies reflected in the waters
And, in our galaxy
The most beautiful was that blue-coloured planet!

The smaller energy
Turned to see a burnt-out piece of earth revolving
     around
It was about to fall at any time into the Sun
Once more, with a flutter of light, it spoke
And then, who knows how,
Life infected the earth!
Bit by bit
Life swallowed up the earth!

पानी की आदत है बहना

पानी की आदत है बहना, बहते रहना
पैर नहीं टिकते दरया के!
दौड़ दौड़ के चट्टानों से
झरने कूदते रहते हैं सब
आबषार पहाड़ पकड़ के नीचे उतरते हैं
थक जाता है दौड़ते भागते, बहता पानी
झील में जाकर नींद आती है पानी को!!

Flowing Water

It is the habit of water to flow, to keep flowing
A river just does not know how to pause!
Bounding across mountain cliffs
All these springs leap about
Holding on to mountains, coming down waterfalls!
But this flowing water gets tired of running all the time
Sleep overtakes it when it enters a lake.

Gulzar

थंपू–भूटान

पिछली बार भी आया था तो . . . इसी पहाड़ ने . . .
नीचे खड़ा था मुझ ये कहा था
तुम लोगों के क़द क्यों छोटे होते हैं? (रह जाते हैं!)

आओ, हाथ पकड़ लो मेरा . . .
पसलियों पर पांव रखो, ऊपर आ जाओ . . .
आओ ठीक से चेहरा तो देखूं तुम कैसे लगते हो (क्या है?)
जैसे मेरी च्युंटियों को तुम, अलग अलग पहचान नहीं सकते
मुझको भी तुम एक ही जैसे लगते हो सब
एक ही फ़र्क़ है
मेरी कोई च्युंटी (जो) बदन पर चढ़ जाए तो
चुटकी से पकड़ के, फेंक के उसको
मार दिया करते हो तुम
मैं ऐसा नहीं करता!

मेरे सनोबर देखो कितने ऊंचे ऊंचे क़द हैं उनके
तुम से सात गुना तो होंगे (शायद दस या बारह गुना हों)
उम्रें देखो उसकी तुम, कितनी बड़ी हैं (सदियों ज़िंदा रहते हैं)
कह देते हो कहने को तुम
लेकिन अपने बड़ों की इज़्ज़त करते नहीं तुम
(इसीलिए तुम लोगों के क़द . . . इतने छोटे रह जाते हैं)

Return to Thimphu

When I had come last time, this very mountain
Had said to me, as I stood below:
Why do you people remain so stunted?

Come, hold my hand
Put your foot on my ribs, come up,
Come, let me at least see what you look like;
Just as you cannot recognize my ants individually
You all seem the same to me
With one difference:
If one of my ants climbs on your body
You catch it by your fingers, throw it off
And kill it
I don't do that!

Look at my pines, how high they soar
They must be at least ten or twelve times your size
Look at their age, how much older they are
You say it for the sake of it
But, actually, you do not respect your elders!

इतना अकेला नहीं हूं मैं, तुम जितना समझते हो;
(तुम ही लोग हो भीड़ में रह कर भी तन्हा तन्हा लगते हो)
भरे हुए जब क़ाफ़ले बादलों के जाते हैं
जफ्फा डाल के मिल कर जाते हैं वो मुझ से

दरया भी उतरते हैं तो पांव छू के
                          विदा होते हैं
मौसम मेरे महमान हैं, आते हैं तो महीनों रह कर जाते हैं
                          अज़ल अज़ल के रिश्ते निभाते हैं

तुम लोगों की उम्रें देखता हूं . . .
कितनी छोटी छोटी मियादों में तुम, मिलते और बिछड़ते हो
ख़्वाहिशें और उम्मीदें भी बस,
          छोटी छोटी उम्रों जितनी . . .
इसीलिए किया . . . तुम लोगों के क़द इतने छोटे रह जाते हैं?

I am not so alone as you may think I am
It is you all who are lonely even in a crowd
When the caravans of clouds come by
They always hug me when we meet.

Even the rivers touch my feet before they leave
The seasons are my guests
When they come they stay for months
Fulfilling a relationship that began with time.

When I see the length of how long you live
What limited horizons define you, your unions and
      partings—
Your desires and ambitions are small
Just like your age-spans
Is that why your sizes remain so stunted?

Scan QR code to access the
Penguin Random House India website